THIS BOOK BELONGS TO

- -

Start Planning Your Trip To Oklahoma

Oklahoma is a beautiful state famous for its mountain ranges, natural parks, and lakes, as well as its cultural and historical significance in frontier history and Native American legacy alike. It is also known as the Sooner State and its name is derived from two Choctaw words.

These words are "humma", which translates to "red", and "okla", which translates to people, meaning the state's literal translation is "red people". Oklahoma is filled with numerous different kinds of attractions.

Its strange extreme weather doesn't stop it from being an incredibly popular location for tourists, promising rich culture, lovely verdancy, ancient rock formations, historical museums, and unique mansions and homes.

Oklahoma is a great choice for a vacation, providing a great mix of natural attractions, historical sites, artistic delights, one-of-a-kind locations, and virtually anything else in between!

It's as good a reason as any to make Oklahoma your next destination for a great holiday!

It's a true staple of the American West and a representation of all that this aesthetic stands for – and yet, it manages to contain something for just about anyone?

So, what is there to do in the Sooner State?

Here are our picks for 50 fun things to do and places to visit in Oklahoma.

Happy Adventure.

Your feedback means a lot for us!

Please, Consider leaving us "5 stars" on your Amazon review.

Thank You!

Copyright © 2022. Akeem Press. All Rights Reserved

No part of this book may be reproduced or transmitted in any form or by any means, electronic or mechanical, including photocopying recording or by any other form without written permission from the publisher.

L.P	PLACES TO GO	LOCATION	EST.	VISITED
1	Philbrook Museum of Art	Tulsa	1939	
2	Oklahoma City National Memorial & Museum	Oklahoma City	1997	
3	Science Museum Oklahoma	Oklahoma City	1958	
4	National Cowboy & Western Heritage Museum	Oklahoma City	1955	
5	Oklahoma City Museum of Art	Oklahoma City	2002	
6	Route 66	Oklahoma-U.S	1926	
7	Beavers Bend State Resort Park	Broken Bow	1937	
8	Myriad Botanical Gardens	Oklahoma City	1971	
9	Henry Overholser Mansion	Oklahoma City	1903	
10	Oklahoma City Zoo and Botanical Garden	Oklahoma City	1902	
11	45th Infantry Division Museum	Oklahoma City	1965	
12	Museum of Osteology	Oklahoma City	2010	
13	Oklahoma Aquarium	Jenks	2003	
14	E.W. Marland Mansion	Ponca City	1928	
15	Wichita Mountains National Wildlife Refuge	Indiahoma	1901	
16	Factory Obscura Mix-Tape	Oklahoma City	2019	
17	Gilcrease Museum	Tulsa	1943	
18	The Cave House of Tulsa	Tulsa	1924	
19	Woolaroc Museum & Wildlife Preserve	Bartlesville	1925	
20	Museum of the Great Plains	Lawton	1961	
21	Robbers Cave State Park	Wilburton	1929	
22	The Center of the Universe	Tulsa	2013	
23	Turner Falls Park	Davis	1868	
24	Lake Murray State Park	Ardmore	2001	
25	The Toy and Action Figure Museum	Pauls Valley	2005	
26	Sam Noble Museum of Natural History	Norman	1899	
27	Old Route 66 Filling Station	Arcadia	1915	
28	J.M. Davis Arms & Historical Museum	Claremore	....	
29	Chickasaw Cultural Center	Sulphur	2010	
30	Ed Galloway's Totem Pole Park	Chelsea	1937	
31	Natural Falls State Park	Colcord	....	
32	Lake Wister State Park	Wister	1946	
33	The American Pigeon Museum	Oklahoma City	1973	
34	Lake Hefner Park	Oklahoma City	1947	
35	Will Rogers Memorial Museum	Claremore	1938	
36	Tiger Safari	Tuttle	2002	
37	Gloss Mountain State Park	Fairview	1977	
38	Oklahoma Route 66 Museum	Clinton	1995	
39	American Banjo Museum	Oklahoma City	1988	
40	Roman Nose State Park	Watonga	1937	
41	Keystone State Park	Derry	1966	
42	The Outsiders House Museum	Tulsa	2017	
43	Lake Tenkiller	Cookson	1947	
44	Tucker Tower	Ardmore	1933	
45	Black Kettle National Grassland	Cheyenne	1960	
46	Chickasaw National Recreation Area	Sulphur	1902	
47	Clayton Lake State Park	Clayton	1965	
48	Deep Fork National Wildlife Refuge	Henryetta	1993	
49	Fort Cobb State Park	Fort Cobb	1958	
50	Fort Smith National Historic Site	Fort Smith	1961	

Inventory

- [ ] Binoculars
- [ ] Bear Spray
- [ ] Cell Phone + Charger
- [ ] Camera + Accessories
- [ ] First aid kit
- [ ] Flashlight / Headlamp
- [ ] Fleece / Waterproof Jacket
- [ ] Guide Book
- [ ] Hand Lotion
- [ ] Hiking Shoes
- [ ] Hand Sanitizer
- [ ] Insect Repellent
- [ ] Lip Balm
- [ ] Medications & Painkillers
- [ ] Maps
- [ ] Ticket / Pass
- [ ] Snacks
- [ ] Sunglasses
- [ ] Spare Socks
- [ ] Sunscreen
- [ ] Sun Hat
- [ ] Trash Bags
- [ ] Toilet Paper
- [ ] Walking Stick
- [ ] Water

- [ ] Sport Shoes
- [ ] Swim Wear
- [ ] Towel
- [ ] Rainproof Backpack Cover
- [ ] Pendrive
- [ ] Powerbank
- [ ] Laptop
- [ ] Small Tripod
- [ ] Phone Holder
- [ ] Extender Cable
- [ ] Bulbs / Fuses
- [ ] Scissors
- [ ] Tent
- [ ] Trash Bags
- [ ] Umbrella
- [ ] National Park Maps
- [ ] National Park Maps
- [ ] Cosmetics
- [ ] Passport / Photocopy
- [ ] ID Card
- [ ] Driver's License
- [ ] ATM Cards
- [ ] Cash
- [ ] Green Card
- [ ] Tool Box

Philbrook Museum of Art

VISTED DATE :	SPRING ○ SUMMER ○ FALL ○ WINTER ○
WEATHER :	☀ ○ ⛅ ○ 🌧 ○ 🌨 ○ ⛈ ○ 💨 ○ TEMP :
FEE(S) :	RATING : ☆ ☆ ☆ ☆ ☆ WILL I RETURN? YES / NO
LODGING :	WHO I WENT WITH :

Description / Things to do :

The Philbrook Museum of Art is an art museum and cultural center that has two properties in Tulsa.

The main museum is located in a 1920s Italian Renaissance villa that was home to Oklahoma oil man Waite Phillips and his wife.

The home itself is impressive, however the art collection is one of the best in the state.

The pieces span European, American, Modern, and Contemporary art and design as well as African, Asian, and Native American genres and reflects contributions from many well-known artists.

The museum is home to a museum shop, event space, library, children's area, and special exhibition space.

The museum also has a satellite gallery in the downtown Tulsa Brady Arts District.

Address: 2727 S. Rockford Road, Tulsa, OK 74114, United States

Passport stamps:

NOTES:

Oklahoma City National Memorial and Museum

Visted date: Spring ◯   Summer ◯   Fall ◯   Winter ◯

Weather: ☀ ◯   ⛅ ◯   🌧 ◯   ❄ ◯   ⛈ ◯   💨 ◯   🌡 **Temp:**

Fee(s):   **Rating:** ☆ ☆ ☆ ☆ ☆   **Will I return?** YES / NO

Lodging: **Who I went with:**

Description / Things to do:

The Oklahoma City National Memorial and Museum is a moving tribute to the victims, survivors, and rescuers who were touched by the tragic Oklahoma City bombing that occurred April 19, 1995.

The memorial sits on the former site of the Alfred P. Murrah Federal Building in downtown Oklahoma City.

The original building was destroyed in the bombing.

The memorial is framed by two twin bronze gates that are stamped with times denoting the minute just before the attack happened and the minute just after.

There is a reflecting pool, a survivor wall, and 168 empty chairs with names inscribed on them to represent each of the victims of the attack.

Address: 620 N. Harvey Avenue, Oklahoma City, OK 73102

Passport stamps:

NOTES:

Science Museum Oklahoma

VISTED DATE: SPRING ◯   SUMMER ◯   FALL ◯   WINTER ◯

WEATHER: ☀ ◯   ⛅ ◯   🌧 ◯   🌨 ◯   ⛈ ◯   💨 ◯   TEMP:

FEE(S):   RATING: ☆ ☆ ☆ ☆ ☆   WILL I RETURN?   YES / NO

LODGING: WHO I WENT WITH:

Description / Things to do:

The Science Museum Oklahoma is a science museum and planetarium in Oklahoma City that features several sections displaying a variety of interesting objects.

The Destination Space exhibit houses the planetarium as well as various items honoring contributions that Oklahomans have made to air and space travel.

The exhibit includes the Oklahoma Aviation and Space Hall of Fame.

In addition, the International Gymnastics Hall of Fame resides in the Science Museum and features a large collection of medals, gymnastics apparatus, sculptures, and more.

The museum also features a 20,000-square-foot kid-friendly area known as CurioCity, which offers learning opportunities through play.

Adsress: 2020 Remington Place, Oklahoma City, OK 73111

Passport stamps:

Notes:

National Cowboy and Western Heritage Museum

VISTED DATE :		SPRING ○	SUMMER ○	FALL ○	WINTER ○
WEATHER :	☀ ○ ⛅ ○ 🌧 ○ 🌨 ○ ⛈ ○ 💨 ○				TEMP :
FEE(S) :	RATING : ☆ ☆ ☆ ☆ ☆			WILL I RETURN?	YES / NO
LODGING :		WHO I WENT WITH :			

DESCRIPTION / THINGS TO DO :

The National Cowboy & Western Heritage Museum is dedicated to Western culture, history, and art.

The museum preserves and displays a large collection of historical and cultural artifacts and pieces of art related to the American West, featuring artists such as Frederic Remington, Charles M. Russell, and James Earle Fraser.

The museum includes an interactive town that reflects life in the West as it was in the early 1900s and has a restaurant and a museum store that sells Western apparel, gifts, books, and souvenirs.

The museum welcomes artists to come and sketch in their galleries and even offers supplies on loan at the visitor services desk.

Address: 1700 NE 63rd Street, Oklahoma City, OK 73111, United States

PASSPORT STAMPS:

NOTES:

Oklahoma City Museum of Art

Visted date: Spring ◯   Summer ◯   Fall ◯   Winter ◯

Weather: ☀ ◯   ⛅ ◯   🌧 ◯   🌨 ◯   ⛈ ◯   💨 ◯   🌡 **Temp:**

Fee(s):   **Rating:** ☆ ☆ ☆ ☆ ☆   **Will I return?**   Yes / No

Lodging: **Who I went with:**

Description / Things to do:

The Oklahoma City Museum of Art is one of the fun places to go for art-lovers, boasting the title of one of the region's most prestigious institutions of art.

It sits in the Donald W. Reynolds Visual Arts Center and features a dynamic mix of permanent and temporary exhibits, as well as film screenings of independent, classic, and foreign films.

The Oklahoma City Museum of Art largely showcases the work of Dale Chihuly by housing one of the world's biggest collections of his glassworks.

The greatest is the jaw-dropping Eleanor Blake Kirkpatrick Memorial Tower that can be seen in the atrium, spanning 55 feet of awe-inspiring vibrant twists of glass.

Other things you can check out at this museum are the works of American and European artists of the 19th and 20th centuries, spanning mediums such as photographs, paintings, sculptures, prints, and more.

Expect to see the creations of the likes of Paul Reed, Renoir and Gustave Courbet, Brett Weston, Georgia O-Keeffe. For a small museum, it sure has a lot to offer!

Address: 415 Couch Dr, Oklahoma City, OK 73102, United States

Passport stamps:

Notes:

Route 66

VISTED DATE :	SPRING ○ SUMMER ○ FALL ○ WINTER ○
WEATHER :	☀ ○ ⛅ ○ 🌧 ○ 🌨 ○ ⛈ ○ 💨 ○ TEMP :
FEE(S) :	RATING : ☆ ☆ ☆ ☆ ☆ WILL I RETURN? YES / NO
LODGING :	WHO I WENT WITH :

Description / Things to do :

Wondering what to do in Oklahoma if you have a car that you can use?

One of the top choices you can go for is a trip down the state run of Route 66!

Although the full length of this famous road goes from Los Angeles to Chicago, it also cuts across Oklahoma diagonally from Tulsa to Oklahoma City.

Roadside attractions and landmarks galore can be seen all along the run of Route 66.

You'll see many places to stop and explore on your sightseeing road trip this weekend!

If you've always wanted to take the "Great American Road Trip" that is Route 66 but have found it quite daunting at its length, starting in this state only can give you a taste of that excitement and enjoyment.

Address: OK, United States

Passport stamps:

NOTES:

Beavers Bend State Resort Park

Visted date: _____ Spring ○ Summer ○ Fall ○ Winter ○

Weather: ☀ ○ ⛅ ○ 🌧 ○ 🌨 ○ ⛈ ○ 💨 ○   Temp: _____

Fee(s): _____ Rating: ☆ ☆ ☆ ☆ ☆   Will I return? Yes / No

Lodging: _____ Who I went with: _____

Description / Things to do:

Beavers Bend State Resort Park is one of the most popular parks of its kind in the state, so it's one of the scenic places to add to your list of things to do in Oklahoma.

Whether you're looking for exciting ways to spend your time or just want to do some relaxed sightseeing, this park will provide a tranquil but enriching break from the world's hustle and bustle.

Beavers Bend State Resort Park is situated close to Broken Bow, consisting of the Hochatown State Park within it, too, as well as its own titular space.

Cedar Creek Golf Course and Lakeview Lodge also call this park their home. There are also other events and attractions littered about its large expanse.

Waterways at the Beavers Bend State Resort Park provide opportunities for boating and fishing, and there are campsites for tent-pitchers and RV-drivers alike that are planning a getaway this weekend.

There is also a nature center packed with programs and entertainment for people from all age groups.

You can then explore the rest of the park by hiking, going on hayrides, riding a horse, or watching birds!

Address: 4350 S, OK-259A, Broken Bow, OK 74728, United States

Passport stamps:

NOTES:

Myriad Botanical Gardens

VISTED DATE:	SPRING ○ SUMMER ○ FALL ○ WINTER ○
WEATHER: ☀ ○ ⛅ ○ 🌧 ○ ❄ ○ ⛈ ○ 💨 ○	TEMP:
FEE(S):	RATING: ☆ ☆ ☆ ☆ ☆ WILL I RETURN? YES / NO
LODGING:	WHO I WENT WITH:

Description / Things to do:

The Myriad Botanical Gardens are among Oklahoma City's most captivating and delightful points of interest.

The gardens, set over 17 acres of land, are an urban garden packed with botanical wonder, verdant landscapes, and interactive ways to spend your time across open spaces.

A sunken lake in the Myriad Botanical Gardens is flanked by gardens and artwork, with the centerpiece being the gorgeous Crystal Bridge Tropical Conservatory.

The conservatory houses exotic flora and fauna of all kinds across 13,000 square feet of space.

Of course, there's more than the conservatory at the Myriad Botanical Gardens. An off-leash dog park, a children's garden and playground, a visitor's center, numerous paths for jogging and walking, several splash fountains, and educational programs galore add to the appeal of the lovely and calming space.

Address: 301 W Reno Ave, Oklahoma City, OK 73102, United States

Passport stamps:

Notes:

Henry Overholser Mansion

VISTED DATE :		SPRING ○	SUMMER ○	FALL ○	WINTER ○
WEATHER :	☀ ○ ⛅ ○ 🌧 ○ ❄ ○ ⛈ ○ 💨 ○				TEMP :
FEE(S) :	RATING : ☆ ☆ ☆ ☆ ☆			WILL I RETURN?	YES / NO
LODGING :		WHO I WENT WITH :			

Description / Things to do :

The Henry Overholser Mansion was built by Oklahoma City founder Henry Overholser in 1903.

It is thought to be the city's first constructed mansion, so it's one of the best tourist attractions for individuals who love history and want to immerse themselves in the city's early years.

The Henry Overholser Mansion was constructed in the Victorian style and boasts an impressive 20 rooms across three floors.

Fittingly, it sits on Heritage Hills, and it has all its original fixtures, furniture, and decor, all preserved meticulously by the local historical society.

It is also rumored to be haunted if you're interested in that!

Address: 405 NW 15th St, Oklahoma City, OK 73103, United States

Passport stamps:

NOTES :

Oklahoma City Zoo and Botanical Garden

VISTED DATE :	SPRING ◯ SUMMER ◯ FALL ◯ WINTER ◯	
WEATHER : ☀ ◯ ⛅ ◯ 🌧 ◯ 🌨 ◯ ⛈ ◯ 💨 ◯	TEMP :	
FEE(S) :	RATING : ☆ ☆ ☆ ☆ ☆	WILL I RETURN? YES / NO
LODGING :	WHO I WENT WITH :	

Description / Things to do :

Termed as one of the best vacation spots, the Oklahoma City Zoo and Botanical Garden is easily among the top 10 most fun spots to check out for animal lovers and nature enthusiasts alike.

It has more than 500 different species of animals, including 100 of which are native to the state, carefully arranged throughout 11 unique "zones" and sections that are easy to navigate.

Operational for over a hundred years, the Oklahoma City Zoo and Botanical Garden will give you the chance to get up close and personal with certain animals through behind-the-scenes events, and there are activities like feedings, shows, demonstrations, and touch tanks to check out.

There are even some enclosures that you can safely walk through, and there are rides on trains and boats to bring you around more easily! The animals you can expect to see at the zoo are lions, tigers, gorillas, rhinos, wallabies, giraffes, lorikeets, Komodo dragons, stingrays, elephants, bears, red pandas, and more.

You'll also get to feast your eyes on habitats mimicking the Ozark Highlands, Turner Falls, the Black Mesa, and beyond. Don't forget to peruse the botanical garden section, too.

Address: 2000 Remington Pl, Oklahoma City, OK 73111, United States

Passport stamps:

Notes :

45th Infantry Division Museum

Visted date: Spring ○   Summer ○   Fall ○   Winter ○

Weather: ☀ ○   ⛅ ○   🌧 ○   ❄ ○   ⛈ ○   💨 ○   **Temp:**

Fee(s):   **Rating:** ☆ ☆ ☆ ☆ ☆   **Will I return?**   YES / NO

Lodging: **Who I went with:**

Description / Things to do:

The 45th Infantry Division Museum is, as its name suggests, devoted to the National Guard's 45th Infantry Division, known as the Thunderbirds.

It is one of the most interesting Oklahoma attractions for those interested in the military and its history and contains 27,000 square feet of space.

It is situated in Oklahoma City.

The 45th Infantry was one of the first units of National Guards sent out for World War II, during which they made an extensive tour of many parts of Europe.

They would go on to serve in the Korean War.

Among the most significant pieces in the 45th Infantry Division Museum's collection are the Reaves Firearm Collection, which is host to a huge range of weapons that date from the Revolutionary War all the way to the Vietnam War, and a genuine Confederate cannon.

Beyond that, other notable features are a collection of over 200 cartoons from a World War II soldier in the 45th Division, an exhibit on the history of flags, a wide range of military history artifacts, and some items from Hitler's apartments.

Address: 2145 NE 36th St, Oklahoma City, OK 73111, United States

Passport stamps:

NOTES :

Museum of Osteology

VISTED DATE :	SPRING ◯ SUMMER ◯ FALL ◯ WINTER ◯
WEATHER :	☀◯ ⛅◯ 🌧◯ 🌨◯ ⛈◯ 💨◯ TEMP :
FEE(S) :	RATING : ☆ ☆ ☆ ☆ ☆ WILL I RETURN? YES / NO
LODGING :	WHO I WENT WITH :

Description / Things to do :

The Museum of Osteology is a privately owned museum showcasing the study of skeletons and bones.

The museum has more than 350 skeletons, including bones from a diverse collection of animals from all the corners of the world.

The museum's exhibits focus on the anatomy and physiology of the skeletal system and displays include taxonomic and educational displays from all five classes of vertebrates.

The collection includes around 5,000 items from 2,500 species. Some of the skeletons on display include elephants, primates, a pygmy sperm whale, an African lion attacking an antelope, and a display of skeletons from local Oklahoma wildlife.

Address: 10301 S. Sunnylane Road, Oklahoma City, OK 73160

Passport stamps:

NOTES:

Oklahoma Aquarium

VISTED DATE:		SPRING ◯ SUMMER ◯ FALL ◯ WINTER ◯	
WEATHER:	☀ ◯ ⛅ ◯ 🌧 ◯ 🌨 ◯ ⛈ ◯ 💨 ◯		🌡 TEMP:
FEE(S):	RATING: ☆ ☆ ☆ ☆ ☆	WILL I RETURN?	YES / NO
LODGING:		WHO I WENT WITH:	

Description / Things to do:

The Oklahoma Aquarium is a huge institution spanning 72,000 square feet, located close to Tulsa in the town of Jenks.

It boasts eight exhibits that showcase a mix of local and exotic marine and ocean wildlife, with a total of 100 different exhibits to peruse.

The Oklahoma Aquarium is famous for having the planet's biggest bullhead shark collection, which can be found in the special Shark Adventure exhibit.

Of course, there are plenty of other fun things to see besides that.

A local aquatic exhibit showcases local marine life and an alligator snapping turtle that is 120 years old.

And colorful creatures can be seen in sections like Eco Zone, Extreme Fishing, Hayes Family Ozark Stream, Polynesian Reef, and Sea Turtle Island.

Address: 300 Aquarium Dr, Jenks, OK 74037, United States

Passport stamps:

NOTES:

E. W. Marland Mansion

Visted date: Spring ○   Summer ○   Fall ○   Winter ○

Weather: ☀ ○   ⛅ ○   🌧 ○   🌨 ○   ⛈ ○   💨 ○   🌡 **Temp:**

Fee(s):   **Rating:** ☆ ☆ ☆ ☆ ☆   **Will I return?** Yes / No

Lodging: **Who I went with:**

Description / Things to do:

The E.W. Marland Mansion was named for a strange, eccentric, ingenious, and complicated individual. The oil magnate, politician, and billionaire set out to create a totally unique mansion home and selected land on the edge of what was once a quarry pit as its site. Then he took all the rocks within the quarry and set out to create an extremely creative and expensive 43,561-square-foot home. The E.W. Marland Mansion has many of the standard lavish fixings, such as crystal chandeliers and marble floors in checked patterns, but what makes it one of the places to visit in Oklahoma are the more unusual features that it boasts.

Apart from its impressive and imposing exterior, it features gorgeously manicured gardens all around the building and a swimming pool carved out from the old quarry itself. Inside the E.W. Marland Mansion, you're in for a treat. The ceilings of the structure are entirely hand-painted one by one, a feat accomplished over the course of three years by Vincent Maragliotti, an Italian muralist flown in specially by Marland.

Motifs of dragons and angels are both proudly displayed and subtly hidden throughout, mosaics of 24 karat gold leaf glisten in the light, and Marland's lifestyle is clearly shown through the beautiful and authentic atmosphere. In addition to that, the E. W. Marland Mansion has a large number of "micro-museums" situated all around the house and the grounds. Various different buildings on the property are dedicated to a wide range of unique and interesting topics, so you'll get to see and experience more than just the house with a single trip! It's easy to see why this is one of Oklahoma's top locations!

Address: 901 Monument Rd, Ponca City, OK 74604, United States

Passport stamps:

NOTES:

Wichita Mountains National Wildlife Refuge

Visted date: Spring ◯   Summer ◯   Fall ◯   Winter ◯

Weather: ☀️◯ ⛅◯ 🌧️◯ 🌨️◯ ⛈️◯ 💨◯   **Temp:**

Fee(s):   **Rating:** ☆ ☆ ☆ ☆ ☆   **Will I return?** Yes / No

Lodging: **Who I went with:**

Description / Things to do:

The Wichita Mountains National Wildlife Refuge, established in 1901, is one of Oklahoma's prettiest places, making it among the best spots across the state for sightseeing.

It is located in the state's southwest area, close to Lawton, and sits between two ranges of granite mountain.

The 59,000-acre expense was once part of a prairie of mixed grass.

Within the Wichita Mountains National Wildlife Refuge are many unique places to see and plenty of activities to try out.

There are trails spanning 15 miles of scenery, multiple lakes full of fish to try catching, and a gorgeous Charon's Garden Wilderness Area for camping and relaxation.

Wildlife, including the biggest land mammal in America, the bison, can be seen wandering throughout the Wichita Mountains National Wildlife Refuge, too!

Address: 32 Refuge Headquarters Road, Indiahoma, OK 73552, United States

Passport stamps:

NOTES :

Factory Obscura Mix-Tape

VISTED DATE:		SPRING ○	SUMMER ○	FALL ○	WINTER ○
WEATHER:	☀ ○ ⛅ ○ 🌧 ○ 🌨 ○ ⛈ ○ 💨 ○			TEMP:	
FEE(S):	RATING: ☆ ☆ ☆ ☆ ☆		WILL I RETURN?	YES / NO	
LODGING:		WHO I WENT WITH:			

Description / Things to do:

The Factory Obscura Mix-Tape was once Automobile Alley's Studebaker Building. In the year 2011, the Flaming Lips rented the brick building, and then, without receiving permits or even asking for the landlord's permission, they completely renovated the building overnight!

The result was a garish, gaudy, and vaguely lewd eyesore of explosive vibrancy, silly artwork, and fun, risque motifs.

Lead singer Wayne Coyne announced that the building was to be converted into an art gallery, which he dubbed the Womb.

Needless to say, the sight became an icon and cemented itself as one of the key choices for what to see in Oklahoma, especially for those who love modern, wild art.

It has video sets, a gallery space, a huge disco ball over a floor of glitter, plenty of parties, and even a gift store and a creative agency.

The Womb was eventually renamed the Mix-Tape and provides an exciting and entertaining sensory art experience across 6,000 square feet.

You'll get to punch a bunch of buttons on a huge tape player and explore all kinds of unique spaces, tunnels, nooks, and interactive spaces.

Address: 25 NW 9th St, Oklahoma City, OK 73102, United States

Passport stamps:

NOTES:

Gilcrease Museum

VISTED DATE :		SPRING ○ SUMMER ○ FALL ○ WINTER ○
WEATHER :	☀ ○ ⛅ ○ 🌧 ○ 🌨 ○ ⛈ ○ 🌬 ○	🌡 TEMP :
FEE(S) :	RATING : ☆ ☆ ☆ ☆ ☆	WILL I RETURN? YES / NO
LODGING :	WHO I WENT WITH :	

Description / Things to do :

The Gilcrease Museum is located in Tulsa, Oklahoma, and is a must-see for those interested in American Western art, as it holds the world's biggest collection of that subject matter!

The museum's property takes up a shocking 460 acres of Osage Hills space and houses 23 acres of themed gardens and a building full of manuscripts, artifacts, and art from Native American culture and frontier settlement history.

The Gilcrease Museum earned its name from Thomas Gilcrease, who donated his art collection to Tulsa upon his passing. He was an oil magnate.

The museum's collection has continued to grow ever since, collecting works from across Latin America.

There are also three areas of the museum specifically made with interactive and creative kids' exhibits!

Address: 1400 N Gilcrease Museum Rd, Tulsa, OK 74127, United States

Passport stamps:

NOTES:

The Cave House of Tulsa

Visted date:		Spring ◯	Summer ◯	Fall ◯ Winter ◯
Weather:	☀ ◯ ⛅ ◯ 🌧 ◯ 🌨 ◯ ⛈ ◯ 💨 ◯			🌡 Temp:
Fee(s):	Rating: ☆ ☆ ☆ ☆ ☆		Will I return?	Yes / No
Lodging:		Who I went with:		

Description / Things to do:

The Cave House of Tulsa is one of Oklahoma's best points of interest, and it's among the state's most interesting places.

It is a unique home decorated by its owners, a mother-daughter pair named Lina and Kate Collier.

The furnishings and decorations are mostly made from all sorts of found and recycled items.

With a lot of different, mysterious rooms in the cave-like structure of the house, The Cave House of Tulsa is a fascinating place to explore.

With jagged bumps and "stalactites", walls of curved stucco, and unusual textures, it's no wonder that it attracts so many visitors!

The Cave House is rumored to be haunted and, in its old days in the 1920s, it was actually a restaurant popular during the Prohibition among outlaws.

It's even said that secret tunnels underground lead to haunted caverns!

Address: 1623 Charles Page Blvd, Tulsa, OK 74127, United States

---

Passport stamps:

NOTES:

Woolaroc Museum and Wildlife Preserve

VISTED DATE:	SPRING ○ SUMMER ○ FALL ○ WINTER ○
WEATHER: ☀ ○ ⛅ ○ 🌧 ○ 🌨 ○ ⛈ ○ 💨 ○	TEMP:
FEE(S):	RATING: ☆ ☆ ☆ ☆ ☆ WILL I RETURN? YES / NO
LODGING:	WHO I WENT WITH:

Description / Things to do:

The Woolaroc Museum & Wildlife Preserve is a whopping 3,700-acre expanse of a verdant, gorgeous landscape.

It is often called Woolaroc Ranch due to the kinds of animals you can see here, like elk, bison, and longhorn cattle, all roaming free and easy to photograph from vehicles.

But what about the museum portion of the Woolaroc Museum & Wildlife Preserve?

Well, it showcases Native American artifacts, Colt firearms, and Western art which are fun to peruse and learn about.

Beyond that, the wide grounds are packed with calming tourist attractions like rocky cliffs, woods, and lakes, with all Oklahoma's history and charm.

Address: 1925 Woolaroc Ranch Rd, Bartlesville, OK 74003, United States

Passport stamps:

Notes :

Museum of the Great Plains

VISTED DATE :		SPRING ○	SUMMER ○ FALL ○	WINTER ○
WEATHER :	☀ ○ ⛅ ○ 🌧 ○ 🌨 ○ ⛈ ○ 💨 ○			🌡 TEMP :
FEE(S) :	RATING : ☆ ☆ ☆ ☆ ☆		WILL I RETURN?	YES / NO
LODGING :		WHO I WENT WITH :		

DESCRIPTION / THINGS TO DO :

THE MUSEUM OF THE GREAT PLAINS IS SITUATED IN LAWTON, OKLAHOMA, AND IT SHOULD BE ON YOUR LIST OF WHERE TO GO IF YOU LIKE NATURAL HISTORY AND CULTURAL HERITAGE.

IT IS PACKED WITH ALL SORTS OF INTERACTIVE EXHIBITS THAT DISCUSS WHAT LIFE WAS LIKE FOR PIONEERS AND NATIVE AMERICANS IN THE WEST.

OUTSIDE OF THE MAIN BUILDING OF THE MUSEUM OF THE GREAT PLAINS, YOU'LL SPOT A WIDE RANGE OF NATURAL HISTORY EXHIBITS IN THE FORM OF BUILDINGS, NAMELY A SCHOOLHOUSE, TRAIN DEPOT, AND TRADING POST.

ADDRESS: 601 NW FERRIS AVE, LAWTON, OK 73507, UNITED STATES

PASSPORT STAMPS:

NOTES :

Robbers Cave State Park

Visted date: Spring ○ Summer ○ Fall ○ Winter ○

Weather: ☀ ○ ⛅ ○ 🌧 ○ 🌨 ○ ⛈ ○ 💨 ○   **Temp:**

Fee(s):   **Rating:** ☆ ☆ ☆ ☆ ☆   **Will I return?** Yes / No

Lodging: **Who I went with:**

Description / Things to do:

Robbers Cave State Park is one of the most beautiful places among Southeast Oklahoma attractions.

It is so named because there is a cave in the park that was used by criminals Jesse James and Belle Starr as a hideout.

Robbers Cave State Park is located in the San Bois Mountains foothills and is packed with beautiful forest and recreational activities, with three lakes, places to hike or ride, and rock climbing spots.

It's also got one of the best spots for ATV-lovers, children, and campers, with facilities for tent-pitchers, RV-drivers, and families with kids of all ages, as well as plenty of events every now and then!

Address: 4628 NW 1027th Ave, Wilburton, OK 74578, United States

Passport stamps:

Notes :

The Center of the Universe

VISTED DATE :		SPRING ○	SUMMER ○	FALL ○	WINTER ○

WEATHER : ☀ ○   ⛅ ○   🌧 ○   🌨 ○   ⛈ ○   💨 ○   TEMP :

FEE(S) :   RATING : ☆ ☆ ☆ ☆ ☆   WILL I RETURN?   YES / NO

LODGING :   WHO I WENT WITH :

Description / Things to do :

The Center of the Universe sounds like a big deal, which can mean it's quite strange to see that it is nothing more than a little circle of concrete, set in the center of a brick circle.

Located in Tulsa, this is one of the more unusual things to do in Oklahoma, but that doesn't make it any less fun.

You see, the Center of the Universe is a unique phenomenon that isn't well-known or scientifically understood.

If you were to stand in that concrete circle and produce any kind of noise.

You will hear that noise reverberate and echo back to you at a much louder level than the original sound.

Essentially, it's like an echo chamber that amplifies sound!

What's more, when heard from outside of that circle, anyone standing outside the circle will hear the noises from within as strange and distorted.

Address: 1 S Boston Ave, Tulsa, OK 74103, United States

Passport stamps:

NOTES:

Turner Falls Park

Visted date: Spring ◯   Summer ◯   Fall ◯   Winter ◯

Weather: ☀ ◯   ⛅ ◯   🌧 ◯   🌨 ◯   ⛈ ◯   💨 ◯   **Temp:**

Fee(s):   **Rating:** ☆ ☆ ☆ ☆ ☆   **Will I return?**   Yes / No

Lodging: **Who I went with:**

Description / Things to do:

Turner Falls Park is one of the much-loved spots in Oklahoma, widely considered a sanctuary for locals.

The wild land provides many natural things to see, but the pride and joy of the park is Turner Falls: a waterfall spanning 77 feet into the air and the state's tallest, boasting streams of ice-cold water, lots of campsites, and a fair few caves to explore.

Turner Falls Park is situated within the Arbuckle Mountains and provides lots of beaches, wading areas, and swimming pools of rock.

The waterfall itself forms a lovely pool called Honey Creek above before it falls to the rushing river below.

Address: I-35 &, US-77, Davis, OK 73030, United States

Passport stamps:

NOTES :

Lake Murray State Park

Visted date: Spring ○   Summer ○   Fall ○   Winter ○

Weather: ☀ ○   ⛅ ○   🌧 ○   🌨 ○   ⛈ ○   💨 ○   🌡 **Temp:**

Fee(s):   **Rating:** ☆ ☆ ☆ ☆ ☆   **Will I return?** Yes / No

Lodging: **Who I went with:**

Description / Things to do:

The first state park established in Oklahoma, Lake Murray State Park encompasses approximately 12,500 acres of wilderness, including the 5,700-acre Lake Murray.

The lake is excellent for boating, fishing, and water sports, but visitors who would rather stay on the shore are encouraged to use the park's 1,000 acres of trails, which welcome hikers, horseback riders, and motorized vehicles.

The park also boasts an 18-acre golf course suitable for players of all abilities, a nature center that houses a fascinating collection of fossils and animal skulls, and a 65-foot tower that boasts stunning panoramic views of the park.

Address: 3323 Lodge Rd, Ardmore, OK 73401, United States

Passport stamps:

NOTES:

The Toy and Action Figure Museum

VISTED DATE :		SPRING ○	SUMMER ○	FALL ○	WINTER ○

WEATHER : ☀ ○   ⛅ ○   🌧 ○   🌨 ○   ⛈ ○   💨 ○   🌡 TEMP :

FEE(S) :   RATING : ☆ ☆ ☆ ☆ ☆   WILL I RETURN?   YES / NO

LODGING :   WHO I WENT WITH :

DESCRIPTION / THINGS TO DO :

THE TOY AND ACTION FIGURE MUSEUM IS A FUN AND BRIGHT SPOT LOCATED IN THE QUIET AND CALM LOCATION OF PAUL'S VALLEY, OKLAHOMA.

IT IS ONE OF THE MOST AWESOME PLACES TO GO FOR TOY LOVERS AND COLLECTORS ALIKE, PROVIDING A HUGE COLLECTION OF MORE THAN 13,000 UNIQUE ACTION FIGURES — INCLUDING A SIGNIFICANT NUMBER THAT HAVE NEVER BEEN REMOVED FROM THEIR PACKAGING!

AT THE TOY AND ACTION FIGURE MUSEUM, YOU'LL MAKE YOUR WAY THROUGH MULTIPLE DIFFERENT MUSEUM SECTIONS.

THE BATCAVE ROOM HAS ONLY COLLECTIBLES AND FIGURES RELATED TO THE CAPED CRUSADER AND HIS MANY FRANCHISES.

THE ARTWORK SECTION HOLDS LOCAL ILLUSTRATIONS' CARTOON WORKS.

THE CENTRAL DIORAMA FEATURES SEVERAL THOUSAND ACTION FIGURES FROM ALL SORTS OF DIFFERENT FRANCHISES!

IF YOU STOP BY THE GIFT SHOP, YOU'LL BE ABLE TO PURCHASE SOME FIGURES OF YOUR OWN, TOO.

ADDRESS: 111 S CHICKASAW ST, PAULS VALLEY, OK 73075, UNITED STATES

PASSPORT STAMPS:

NOTES:

Sam Noble Museum of Natural History

VISTED DATE :　　　　　　　　SPRING ○　SUMMER ○　FALL ○　WINTER ○

WEATHER :　☀ ○　⛅ ○　🌧 ○　🌨 ○　⛈ ○　💨 ○　🌡 TEMP :

FEE(S) :　　　　　RATING : ☆ ☆ ☆ ☆ ☆　　　WILL I RETURN?　YES / NO

LODGING :　　　　　　　　　WHO I WENT WITH :

Description / Things to do :

The Sam Noble Museum of Natural History is located within the University of Oklahoma's campus grounds.

It is a showcase of natural history across multiple different topics.

Permanent exhibits include the Hall of Ancient Life, which is packed with numerous brilliant dinosaur skeletons, including the largest skull of a land animal ever found: a Pentaceratops skull.

Other permanent exhibits are the Hall of World Cultures, which has the obvious subject matter of looking into international cultures, and the Discovery Room where people of all ages can interact with a hands-on exhibit of experiences and activities, such as animal feedings.

Temporary exhibits also provide more options for what to do at the Sam Noble Museum of Natural History!

Address: 2401 Chautauqua Ave, Norman, OK 73072, United States

Passport stamps:

Notes:

Old Route 66 Filling Station

Visted date: Spring ◯   Summer ◯   Fall ◯   Winter ◯

Weather: ☀ ◯   ⛅ ◯   🌧 ◯   🌨 ◯   ⛈ ◯   💨 ◯   **Temp:**

Fee(s):   **Rating:** ☆ ☆ ☆ ☆ ☆   **Will I return?**   Yes / No

Lodging: **Who I went with:**

Description / Things to do:

The Old Route 66 Filling Station is a quaint little stop along the best road in America.

It is little more than a skeleton now, and it is believed to date back to 1920.

The stone building was a filling station, but at its busiest, it was also the home of an Oklahoma counterfeiter — or so legend says.

A plaque in front of the Old Route 66 Filling Station tells you all about that aforementioned legend, and sources are hazy — but it's certainly fun to speculate.

During the Great Depression, it is said that a man offered the owner some currency plates, and the owner of the establishment set to work printing bills with that man behind the station.

The small-time criminals were quickly discovered, though, and the station shut down.

For lovers of the obscure and strange, this is a must-do while you're driving down Route 66.

Address: E Danforth Rd/Route 66, Arcadia, OK 73007, United States

---

Passport stamps:

NOTES :

J. M. Davis Arms and Historical Museum

VISTED DATE :   SPRING ○   SUMMER ○   FALL ○   WINTER ○

WEATHER :   ☀ ○   ⛅ ○   🌧 ○   🌨 ○   ⛈ ○   💨 ○   🌡 TEMP :

FEE(S) :   RATING : ☆ ☆ ☆ ☆ ☆   WILL I RETURN?   YES / NO

LODGING :   WHO I WENT WITH :

Description / Things to do :

The J.M. Davis Arms & Historical Museum is a huge privately-owned establishment that both provides historical information and displays on arms and the history of Oklahoma City and the surrounding area.

It contains over 50,000 artifacts, with more than 12,000 being a part of Davis' own firearms collection.

That collection spans as far back as the 14th century and makes the museum one of the greatest tourist spots for gun aficionados.

There is even a gallery of oddities and guns owned by outlaws!

The J.M. Davis Arms & Historical Museum also has a wide range of artifacts from Native American cultures, historic memorabilia from the Wild West, genuine riding saddles, artifacts from World War II, steins, a recreation of the Mason Hotel earned by Davies, instruments, and a huge M41 Walker Bulldog tank from the US Army on display outdoors. If you're lucky, this weekend there may even be a special, fun event on, such as live reenactments of various historical events.

You should also view the Cooweescoowee District of the Nation exhibit, which covers two centuries of Cherokee history.

Address: 330 N J M Davis Blvd, Claremore, OK 74017, United States

Passport stamps:

NOTES :

Chickasaw Cultural Center

Visited date: Spring ○   Summer ○   Fall ○   Winter ○

Weather: ☀ ○   ⛅ ○   🌧 ○   🌨 ○   ⛈ ○   💨 ○   **Temp:**

Fee(s):   **Rating:** ☆ ☆ ☆ ☆ ☆   **Will I return?**   Yes / No

Lodging: **Who I went with:**

Description / Things to do:

The Chickasaw Cultural Center is one of the key tourist attractions to learn about the heritage, history, and culture of the native Chickasaw people.

It is situated fittingly close to the Chickasaw National Recreation Area in Sulphur and is a high-quality, world-class institution for the celebration of this culture.

One of the loved features of the Chickasaw Cultural Center is the Chickasha Poya Exhibit Center, which is an interactive hub of exhibits that are hands-on and inviting for visitors.

This includes a spirit dance showcase, a display of mosaic tiles, and a Spirit Forest.

Outside of the Chickasaw Cultural Center, you'll get to see the Aaholiitobli's Honor Garden.

The garden is a dedication to Chickasaw leaders, warriors, and elders, featuring laser-cut photographs of each individual carefully arranged on the walls of the Chickasaw Nation Hall of Fame.

Address: 867 Cooper Memorial Rd, Sulphur, OK 73086, United States

Passport stamps:

NOTES :

Ed Galloway's Totem Pole Park

VISTED DATE: _____ SPRING ○ SUMMER ○ FALL ○ WINTER ○

WEATHER: ☀ ○ ⛅ ○ 🌧 ○ 🌨 ○ ⛈ ○ 💨 ○   🌡 TEMP: _____

FEE(S): _____   RATING: ☆ ☆ ☆ ☆ ☆   WILL I RETURN? YES / NO

LODGING: _____   WHO I WENT WITH: _____

Description / Things to do:

Ed Galloway's Totem Pole Park is a rather interesting collection of decorations, homemade out of cement by Oklahoma artisan Ed Galloway. He spent several decades crafting this fun location, beginning in 1938 with the goal of creating several totem poles out of strong materials like steel, concrete, and rebar. The result was what we now know as the Totem Pole Park, packed with tapered totems and totem poles in all sorts of different vibrant colors.

The centerpiece is a huge pole that took a whopping 11 years to complete and is so large that it actually has a room inside it that you can go into!

It reaches 90 feet into the air and has 200 or so carved figures in it, ranging from beasts to faces.

Of course, there is some controversy surrounding Ed Galloway's Totem Pole Park, primarily because totem poles are meant to be sacred and traditional monuments of Indigenous Native Americans. They're meant to celebrate and commemorate history, culture, and ancestry and are made from natural materials like red cedar. Still, as an artistic location, you can add Ed Galloway's Totem Pole Park to your list of stuff to do.

The park was almost ruined after the site was left in disrepair after Galloway's passing in 1962, but conservationists saved it and the totem poles are in great shape now.

Address: 21300 OK-28 A, Chelsea, OK 74016, United States

Passport stamps:

NOTES :

Natural Falls State Park

VISTED DATE :   SPRING ○   SUMMER ○   FALL ○   WINTER ○

WEATHER :   ☀ ○   ⛅ ○   🌧 ○   🌨 ○   ⛈ ○   💨 ○   TEMP :

FEE(S) :   RATING : ☆ ☆ ☆ ☆   WILL I RETURN?   YES / NO

LODGING :   WHO I WENT WITH :

Description / Things to do :

If Natural Falls State Park sounds idyllic, that's because it is — and it may be one of Oklahoma's most romantic things to do!

It's also one of the few Oklahoma attractions that sits on the border to Arkansas. The falls in question are 77 feet tall and rush down over a promontory to come to rest in a gorgeous, all-natural pool of cool water.

One of the most interesting features of the Natural Falls State Park is the pool itself, which hosts a unique micro-habitat due to the special climate that the waterfall creates.

Unique plants manage to grow here in a way that you won't find easily elsewhere. The valley, which is V-shaped, has a relaxing atmosphere to boot. At the zenith of the falls, there is a wheelchair-accessible observation platform.

Natural Falls State Park provides the chance to stay overnight in one of five whimsical yurts, each outfitted with modern amenities!

And, of course, fans of Where The Red Fern Grows, the movie from 1974, will appreciate the parts of the park that were used in the film!

Address: 19225 E 578 Rd, Colcord, OK 74338, United States

Passport stamps:

NOTES:

Lake Wister State Park

Visted date: Spring ○   Summer ○   Fall ○   Winter ○

Weather: ☀ ○   ⛅ ○   🌧 ○   🌨 ○   ⛈ ○   💨 ○   🌡 **Temp:**

Fee(s):   **Rating:** ☆ ☆ ☆ ☆   **Will I return?**   Yes / No

Lodging: **Who I went with:**

Description / Things to do:

Occupying 3,428 acres in the southeastern part of the state, Lake Wister State Park serves as a gateway to the 1.8 million-acre Ouachita National Forest.

The biggest attraction in the park is the 7,300-acre Lake Wister, which has several public boat ramps and is perfect for boating, water skiing, and other water sports.

A swimming beach can be found on the shore, as can five campgrounds with sites for both tents and RVs.

When not on the lake, visitors can splash around in the park's water park, visit the nature center, or play a round of golf on the mini golf course.

Address: 25567 US-270, Wister, OK 74966, United States

Passport stamps:

NOTES:

The American Pigeon Museum

Visited date: Spring ◯   Summer ◯   Fall ◯   Winter ◯

Weather: ☀ ◯   ⛅ ◯   🌧 ◯   🌨 ◯   ⛈ ◯   💨 ◯   🌡 **Temp:**

Fee(s):   **Rating:** ☆ ☆ ☆ ☆ ☆   **Will I return?**   YES / NO

Lodging: **Who I went with:**

Description / Things to do:

Looking for more fun things to see?

The American Pigeon Museum in Oklahoma City fits that bill!

While we often laugh at pigeons and even view them as pests, they're actually very intelligent birds — and, once upon a time, they were crucial to long-distance communication.

The American Pigeon Museum began its life as the American Homing Pigeon Institute in 1973 when it was devoted to the simple purpose of pigeon training.

The Institute expanded in 1993 by purchasing 10 acres of land in the city to turn into a World of Wings pigeon center and the museum all at once.

The American Pigeon Museum now houses numerous displays, many named after relevant enthusiasts and researchers, with all sorts of pigeon-related memorabilia. This includes ads, statues, art, "wings", clocks, and informational displays on the importance of homing pigeons during both World Wars. There are even exhibits designed to honor heroic birds!

You'll be impressed by the beauty and rich history of these surprisingly majestic birds.

Address: 2300 NE 63rd St, Oklahoma City, OK 73111, United States

Passport stamps:

NOTES:

Lake Hefner Park

VISTED DATE: SPRING ○ SUMMER ○ FALL ○ WINTER ○

WEATHER: ☀ ○ ⛅ ○ 🌧 ○ 🌨 ○ ⛈ ○ 💨 ○   TEMP:

FEE(S): RATING: ☆ ☆ ☆ ☆ ☆   WILL I RETURN? YES / NO

LODGING: WHO I WENT WITH:

Description / Things to do:

Lake Hefner Park's center is the titular Lake Hefner, a man-made reservoir that was originally created in order to aid the city's issues with water shortages.

It has since turned into one of the most delightful places to visit in Oklahoma for tourists and locals alike.

With 2,500 acres of land to its name, Lake Hefner Park is a haven for water activities like sailing and fishing, and it's also ideal for picnics by the picturesque lake.

The lake has a whopping 18 miles of length in shoreline and 29 feet in depth.

The urban space is outfitted with sports areas like tracks, a golf course, a softball field, a soccer field, and a field for model airplane flight, and there are plenty of modern amenities to make use of, too.

There are also trails for bikes and pedestrians spanning nine miles!

Address: 3301 NW Grand Blvd, Oklahoma City, OK 73116, United States

Passport stamps:

NOTES :

Will Rogers Memorial Museum

VISTED DATE :   SPRING ○ SUMMER ○ FALL ○ WINTER ○

WEATHER :   ☀ ○   ⛅ ○   🌧 ○   ❄ ○   ⛈ ○   💨 ○   TEMP :

FEE(S) :   RATING : ☆ ☆ ☆ ☆ ☆   WILL I RETURN?   YES / NO

LODGING :   WHO I WENT WITH :

Description / Things to do :

The Will Rogers Memorial Museum is one of the surefire places to see for fans of legendary entertainers like the titular Will Rogers.

Located in Claremore, it is a tribute to the famed "Cowboy Philosopher" of America, a product of several discussions on how to honor him upon his passing in 1935.

The Oklahoma Legislature, Betty Rogers (Will's wife), and thousands of donors all worked together to make the Will Rogers Memorial Museum a reality.

It is now the world's biggest collection of artifacts related to Will Rogers and his writings, boasting twelve galleries, a library, a theater, and even a children's museum, all packed with documentaries, memorabilia, manuscripts, photos, speeches, and all of Rogers' writings.

Address: 1720 W Will Rogers Blvd, Claremore, OK 74017, United States

Passport stamps:

NOTES:

Tiger Safari

Visted date :   Spring ○   Summer ○   Fall ○   Winter ○

Weather : ☀ ○   ⛅ ○   🌧 ○   ❄ ○   ⛈ ○   💨 ○   **Temp :**

Fee(s) :   **Rating :** ☆ ☆ ☆ ☆ ☆   **Will I return?**   YES / NO

Lodging :   **Who I went with :**

Description / Things to do :

The Tiger Safari is a fun option for what to do with kids – or animal lovers of any age – in Oklahoma, one of the best places in the US!

Its full name is "Tiger Safari Zoological Park", and it is situated in the lovely locale of Tuttle.

The safari spans 45 acres and is a zoo boasting more than 150 animals, including exotic animals like African wildcats, bears, birds, and reptiles.

Interactive visits at the Tiger Safari let you play games, take part in events, visit a petting zoo, and get close to exotic fauna of all kinds.

The safari is a non-profit organization that doubles as a way of educating the public on caring for exotic creatures, which is a significant step forward since it was created by a husband and wife couple that were simply collecting these creatures.

Address: 963 County Street 2930, Tuttle, OK 73089, United States

Passport stamps:

NOTES :

Gloss Mountain State Park

Visted date: Spring ○   Summer ○   Fall ○   Winter ○

Weather: ☀ ○   ⛅ ○   🌧 ○   ❄ ○   ⛈ ○   💨 ○   **Temp:**

Fee(s):   **Rating:** ☆ ☆ ☆ ☆   **Will I return?** Yes / No

Lodging: **Who I went with:**

Description / Things to do:

Gloss Mountain State Park is one of the loveliest things to do in Oklahoma for nature lovers and outdoor enthusiasts.

The name of the park comes from the Gloss Mountains, often referred to as the Glass Mountains because of their shiny, Selenite surface.

As far as panoramas go, it's a stunning backdrop for park activities like hiking, eating picnics, and photography.

Gloss Mountain State Park is relatively well-outfitted with facilities and provides numerous trails throughout, including one that runs up to Cathedral Mountain.

From the peak of that mountain, you can look around and take in the gorgeous sight of the valley and Lone Peak Mountain beyond!

Address: US-412, Fairview, OK 73737, United States

Passport stamps:

NOTES :

Oklahoma Route 66 Museum

Visted date: Spring ◯   Summer ◯   Fall ◯   Winter ◯

Weather: ☀ ◯   ⛅ ◯   🌧 ◯   🌨 ◯   ⛈ ◯   💨 ◯   **Temp:**

Fee(s):   **Rating:** ☆ ☆ ☆ ☆ ☆   **Will I return?**   Yes / No

Lodging: **Who I went with:**

Description / Things to do:

As far as tourist attractions go, Route 66 is one of America's most renowned, and the Oklahoma Route 66 Museum celebrates that legacy.

It is a spot dedicated to exhibiting music, history, myths, and memorabilia related to the iconic road, dating all the way back to its initial conception and construction.

The Oklahoma Route 66 Museum lets you get up close and personal with the tales of the Mother Road, the music that was created in its time, sounds of the highway and of the events that took place on the road, and more.

There is also a 1950s-style diner onsite for you to try out!

Address: 2229 W Gary Blvd, Clinton, OK 73601, United States

Passport stamps:

NOTES :

American Banjo Museum

Visited date: Spring ○   Summer ○   Fall ○   Winter ○

Weather: ☀ ○   ⛅ ○   🌧 ○   ❄ ○   ⛈ ○   🌬 ○   🌡 **Temp:**

Fee(s):   **Rating:** ☆ ☆ ☆ ☆ ☆   **Will I return?**   Yes / No

Lodging: **Who I went with:**

Description / Things to do:

The American Banjo Museum is home to the world's biggest public display of instruments and is a fun and interesting delve into the history of the delightful, twangy string instrument known as the banjo.

The instrument is widely considered synonymous with the country and cowboy culture, but this museum goes deeper than that to showcase the good, bad, and ugly parts of its history.

The banjo was appropriated in the mid-1600s by American slaves.

Back then, it was made with animal skins and gourds.

Since then, it has become an integral feature in many features of American music, and the American Banjo Museum features more than 300 of them in a wall-to-wall display.

Banjos at the American Banjo Museum range from calibrated banjos used in concerts, traditional handmade folk creations, and ornate banjos from the Jazz era.

Sheet music, out-of-print records, ephemera and memorabilia, and more add color and vibrancy to the museum's offerings!

Address: 9 E Sheridan Ave, Oklahoma City, OK 73104, United States

Passport stamps:

NOTES :

Roman Nose State Park

Visited date: Spring ○   Summer ○   Fall ○   Winter ○

Weather: ☀ ○   ⛅ ○   🌧 ○   🌨 ○   ⛈ ○   💨 ○   **Temp:**

Fee(s):   **Rating:** ☆ ☆ ☆ ☆   **Will I return?**   Yes / No

Lodging: **Who I went with:**

Description / Things to do:

The Roman Nose State Park is one of seven original Oklahoma state parks, and it is named after a Cheyenne chief.

It is undoubtedly a gorgeous location and is among Oklahoma attractions that double as places to vacation, with a huge expanse of land containing all sorts of incredible ways to stay occupied over a prolonged trip.

At the Roman Nose State Park, you can feast your eyes on its breathtaking canyon, any of its beautiful natural springs, and its awe-inspiring cliffs of gypsum rock.

It is outfitted for guests with 11 cabins to rent, the lovely Roman Nose State Park Lodge, campground facilities that are fully outfitted, and bookable teepees.

All sorts of activities are available at the Roman Nose State Park.

Its most notable is the Roman Nose State Park Golf Course, a par 70, 18-hole course that features lovely fairways of Bermuda grass, sloping greens, views of the lake and canyon walls, and all sorts of natural obstacles.

Of course, you can also keep things natural by going fishing, biking, boating, horse riding, hiking, swimming, or simply enjoying a relaxing time in the great outdoors.

Address: 3236 OK-8A, Watonga, OK 73772, United States

Passport stamps:

Notes:

Keystone State Park

VISTED DATE : SPRING ◯ SUMMER ◯ FALL ◯ WINTER ◯

WEATHER : ☀ ◯ ⛅ ◯ 🌧 ◯ 🌨 ◯ ⛈ ◯ 💨 ◯   **TEMP :**

FEE(S) :   **RATING :** ☆ ☆ ☆ ☆ ☆   **WILL I RETURN?** YES / NO

LODGING :   **WHO I WENT WITH :**

Description / Things to do :

Keystone State Park is situated on the beautiful Keystone Lake, which is perfect for swimming, fishing, boating, and water sports.

There are several boat ramps within the park for visitor use, and there is also a marina that offers rental boats, a restaurant, fuel, and a convenience store with groceries and other boating necessities.

The lake might be the biggest attraction in the park, but there are plenty of things to do on the shore as well, including hiking trails, covered picnic areas with grills, and RV and tent campsites.

Visitors can also stay in one of the park's furnished one- and two-bedroom cabins.

Address: 1150 Keystone Park Rd, Derry, PA 15627-3679, United States

PASSPORT STAMPS:

NOTES :

The Outsiders House Museum

VISITED DATE:	SPRING ◯ SUMMER ◯ FALL ◯ WINTER ◯
WEATHER: ☀◯ ⛅◯ 🌧◯ ❄◯ ⛈◯ 💨◯	TEMP:
FEE(S):	RATING: ☆ ☆ ☆ ☆ ☆ WILL I RETURN? YES / NO
LODGING:	WHO I WENT WITH:

Description / Things to do:

The Outsiders House Museum may look familiar to fans and watchers of The Outsiders.

For years, it was the home of the Curtis brothers, and it has now been converted into a museum celebrating the film and the tale that resonated with lives across the globe. It's one of the state's more unique things to see!

Francis Ford Coppola, director of the Outsiders, came to Oklahoma in 1982 and began working on the movie, which is based on a novel from 1967.

The whole film was shot in Tulsa, and the home used was owned privately for years after the movie was released.

When it was abandoned and fell into disrepair, it was purchased by Danny Boy O'Connor, a musician, and with the aid of donations and hard work, the house was fashioned into a museum and opened in 2019.

A tour of the Outsiders House Museum includes a ride to other locations where the Outsiders was filmed within the city.

The museum itself houses books, posters, wardrobe pieces, artifacts, autographed items, and more memorabilia related to the iconic film.

Address: 731 N St Louis Ave, Tulsa, OK 74106, United States

Passport stamps:

NOTES:

Lake Tenkiller

Visted date :	Spring ○ Summer ○ Fall ○ Winter ○
Weather : ☀ ○ ⛅ ○ 🌧 ○ 🌨 ○ ⛈ ○ 💨 ○	Temp :
Fee(s) :	Rating : ☆ ☆ ☆ ☆ ☆ Will I return? Yes / No
Lodging :	Who I went with :

Description / Things to do :

Lake Tenkiller should be on your list of sights to see and places to visit in Oklahoma thanks to its gorgeous environment and calming experience.

It can be exciting for families, romantic for couples, and ideal for a quick getaway.

Known also as Tenkiller Ferry Lake, Lake Tenkiller is situated south of Tahlequah on the Illinois River and is a natural feature of Cookson Hills.

The lake stretches into Cherokee and Sequoyah and provides lots of water-based activity opportunities.

You can fish for crappie, rainbow trout, bass, catfish, and walleye.

You can keep your eyes peeled for doves, geese, squirrels, deer, ducks, quail, and other wildlife.

There are public-use locations for camping and relaxing, and scuba divers will love the clear waters and its multitude of sunken structures to explore.

Address: 446977 E 980 Rd, Cookson, OK 74427, United States

Passport stamps:

NOTES:

Tucker Tower

Visted date:	Spring ○ Summer ○ Fall ○ Winter ○
Weather:	☀ ○ ⛅ ○ 🌧 ○ 🌨 ○ ⛈ ○ 💨 ○ 🌡 Temp:
Fee(s):	Rating: ☆ ☆ ☆ ☆ ☆ Will I return? Yes / No
Lodging:	Who I went with:

Description / Things to do:

Tucker Tower is a beautiful and stately structure in Lake Murray State Park and has unofficial renown for being one of the most easily identifiable structures within a state park of Oklahoma.

It was named after state senator Fred Tucker during its construction in the 1930s and was mostly built and designed by the Works Progress Administration.

Tucker Tower was actually originally meant to be one of the places to go for a retreat for state governors, but that never wound up happening.

It began its life as a geological museum instead and is, today, a nature center for Lake Murray State Park. It has two floors, with the main level housing an exhibit-filled museum with historical and informational displays relating to the tower and the area around it.

The main level also has a patio approximately 60 feet above the surface of a lake. On the second level, accessible via stairs, Tucker Tower rises 65 feet above its lower floor.

A walkway on that level allows you to look around and see stunning views in all directions for miles. It's a great spot for photos, site seeing, and more.

You'll spot Tucker Tower from a distance as it sits on a strand of twisted, craggy rock.

Address: 18407 Scenic Highway 77, Ardmore, OK 73401, United States

Passport stamps:

NOTES:

Black Kettle National Grassland

VISTED DATE :	SPRING ○ SUMMER ○ FALL ○ WINTER ○
WEATHER :	☀ ○ ⛅ ○ 🌧 ○ 🌨 ○ ⛈ ○ 💨 ○ TEMP :
FEE(S) :	RATING : ☆ ☆ ☆ ☆ ☆ WILL I RETURN? YES / NO
LODGING :	WHO I WENT WITH :

Description / Things to do :

Spread out over both Oklahoma and Texas, the Black Kettle National Grassland is made up of approximately one hundred separate tracts of land.

Some of these areas are used for cattle grazing and for energy.

And three of the sites in Oklahoma are open to the public for recreation: Spring Creek Lake, Black Kettle Recreation Area, and Skipout Lake.

All of these sites are open year-round, and they offer excellent opportunities for picnicking, camping, fishing, and hiking.

Visitors who are interested in learning about the area's history can also stroll along the Black Kettle Interpretive Trail or visit the Washita Battlefield National Historic Site.

Address: 18555 U.S. 87A, Cheyenne, OK 73628, United States

Passport stamps:

Notes:

Chickasaw National Recreation Area

Visited date : SPRING ○ SUMMER ○ FALL ○ WINTER ○

Weather : ☀ ○ ⛅ ○ 🌧 ○ 🌨 ○ ⛈ ○ 💨 ○   **Temp :**

Fee(s) :   **Rating :** ☆ ☆ ☆ ☆ ☆   **Will I return?** YES / NO

Lodging :   **Who I went with :**

Description / Things to do :

Tucked away in the foothills of the Arbuckle Mountains.

The Chickasaw National Recreation Area is home to a large assortment of lakes, streams, swimming holes, waterfalls, and mineral springs.

Much of the park is taken up by the 2,350 acre Lake of the Arbuckles, which offers year-round fishing, excellent swimming, and tent and RV camping along the shore.

Visitors are also welcome to swim and fish in many of the park's other bodies of water and hike on the trails that run through the park and around the lake.

No admission fee is charged to enter the park.

Address: 901 W 1st St, Sulphur, OK 73086, United States

Passport stamps:

Notes :

Clayton Lake State Park

VISTED DATE :   SPRING ○ SUMMER ○ FALL ○ WINTER ○

WEATHER :   ☀ ○   ☁ ○   🌧 ○   ❄ ○   ⛈ ○   💨 ○   TEMP :

FEE(S) :   RATING : ☆ ☆ ☆ ☆ ☆   WILL I RETURN?   YES / NO

LODGING :   WHO I WENT WITH :

DESCRIPTION / THINGS TO DO :

Conveniently located only a few miles away from the town of Clayton, Clayton Lake State Park is a 510-acre park that encompasses a beautiful 80-acre lake with a fishing dock and a swimming beach.

Visitors are welcome to use the lake for swimming, boating, and fishing, but water sports are not permitted.

The park also offers plenty of overnight accommodation, including rustic cabins, family-friendly two-bedroom cabins, and RV and tent campsites.

The RV campsites can be reserved, but the tent sites are first-come first-served.

Other park amenities include a children's playground, hiking trails, picnic tables, and covered picnic areas perfect for groups.

Address: 141 Clayton Lake Rd, Clayton, NM 88415, United States

PASSPORT STAMPS:

NOTES :

Deep Fork National Wildlife Refuge

Visited date: Spring ○   Summer ○   Fall ○   Winter ○

Weather: ☀ ○   ⛅ ○   🌧 ○   🌨 ○   ⛈ ○   🌬 ○   Temp:

Fee(s):   Rating: ☆ ☆ ☆ ☆ ☆   Will I return?   Yes / No

Lodging: Who I went with:

Description / Things to do:

Established in 1993, the Deep Fork National Wildlife Refuge was created to protect the forests along the Deep Fork River and the many different types of wildlife that call this area home.

The park is excellent for wildlife viewing and bird watching, and there are approximately 17 miles of trails for visitors to enjoy, including a 1,200-foot trail with an elevated boardwalk.

Other popular activities in the refuge include canoeing and kayaking, fishing, and hunting when in season.

The refuge is open to visitors year-round, and there are several visitor parking areas scattered throughout the property.

Address: 21844 S 250 Rd, Henryetta, OK 74437, United States

Passport stamps:

Notes:

Fort Cobb State Park

VISTED DATE :	SPRING ○ SUMMER ○ FALL ○ WINTER ○
WEATHER :	☀ ○ ⛅ ○ 🌧 ○ ❄ ○ ⛈ ○ 💨 ○ 🌡 TEMP :
FEE(S) :	RATING : ☆ ☆ ☆ ☆ ☆ WILL I RETURN? YES / NO
LODGING :	WHO I WENT WITH :

Description / Things to do :

Sitting on the edge of the 4,000-acre Fort Cobb Lake, Fort Cobb State Park boasts plenty of opportunities for recreation both on and off the water.

The lake is excellent for swimming, boating, water sports, and fishing, and there is a marina with a convenience store, boat and boat slip rentals, a restaurant, and fuel.

Visitors are also welcome to enjoy the park's 18-hole golf course, which includes a driving range and a putting green.

When it comes to accommodation, the park offers approximately 600 campsites for both tents and RVs, some of which are equipped with electrical and water hookups.

Address: 27022 Copperhead Road, Fort Cobb, OK 73038, United States

Passport stamps:

NOTES:

Fort Smith National Historic Site

Visted date: Spring ◯   Summer ◯   Fall ◯   Winter ◯

Weather: ☀ ◯   ⛅ ◯   🌧 ◯   ❄ ◯   ⛈ ◯   💨 ◯   Temp:

Fee(s):   Rating: ☆ ☆ ☆ ☆   Will I return?   Yes / No

Lodging: Who I went with:

Description / Things to do:

Fort Smith was first established in 1817, and the Fort Smith National Historic Site was created in 1861 to protect the fort's remains.

There are plenty of things to see and do at the site, but a major highlight is touring the Visitor's Center.

Which is located inside the fort's old Courthouse building and features plenty of informative exhibits about important pieces of history like the fort's use as a military base and the Trail of Tears.

Self-guided audio tours of both the buildings and the grounds are available, and ranger-led tours are sometimes offered as well.

Address: 301 Parker Ave Fort Smith, AR 72901, United States

Passport stamps:

NOTES :